Tunnel Vision

A play

Sheila Hodgson

Samuel French—London
New York-Toronto-Hollywood

ISBN 0 573 12269 5

Please see page iv for further copyright information

CHARACTERS

Peter Leyland, early 50s
Angie Leyland, late 40s
Susan Leyland, 20s
Brian Medway, young
Liz, teenager

The action of the play takes place in an Underground station

Time: the present

Production Note

The poster illusion on page 34 is simple. A short length of fishing line should be attached to the top right corner of the poster, taken diagonally across and through a small hole in the back flat. A careful pull from behind does the rest.

S.H.

TUNNEL VISION

We are looking at the platform of an Underground station. A plain wall runs along the length of the back with the London Underground distinctive logo printed across the centre, but displaying no station name. There are two vividly coloured posters displayed R and L of the sign and a red plastic bench set against the wall C. A high curved archway R has "EXIT" marked above it; an identical archway L is marked "NO EXIT"

The lighting is harsh and flat, slightly orangey

A teenage girl—Liz—squats on the floor UR. She has her back against the wall and is possibly half asleep. A bulging carrier bag lies on the ground beside her

Angie Leyland comes swiftly through the arch L. In her late forties, she is smartly dressed in clothes a little too young for her, the skirt just a little too short. Angie's manner when in a good mood is girlish; at the moment she is in a bad mood

She is followed by Brian Medway, a placid young man in a sports jacket

Angie …it's not my fault, I don't know why everybody is blaming me, I simply want to get home as fast as possible.

Brian We could have taken a taxi.

Angie Yes, well, that was becoming ridiculous. The two of you leaping up and down hailing everything in sight from a private car to a hearse, for heaven's sake, Brian, we'd been standing there over half an hour and it was starting to rain. Has it wrecked my hair?

Brian No.

Angie Where have they got to now…? (*She sweeps* UL *and peers through the arch* L)

Brian crosses UR *to Liz*

Brian Excuse me.

Liz looks up

Liz Hullo.

Brian Do you happen to know? Will there be a train soon?

Liz (*yawning*) Fifteen minutes.

Brian Oh, that's all right.

Liz Is it hell. I been stuck here since half past ten. I keep asking and you get a different answer every bloody time. The latest is "Fifteen minutes".

Brian (*moving away*) Good. Thank you.

Liz Signal.

Brian Sorry?

Liz There's a signal failure further down the line.

Brian Oh.

Liz Makes you spit, doesn't it?

Angie (*calling*) Hurry up! We may miss the train.

Brian There isn't a train.

Angie (*moving down to him*) Why? Has the last one gone?

Brian No, of course not, they wouldn't have let us in. They lock the entrance gates at night.

Liz Signal.

Angie What?
Liz (*calling across*) Signal. I did tell him.

Peter Leyland enters slowly through the arch L. He is actually in his early fifties but ill health has made him look older. He wears his best suit and is holding on to the arm of his daughter Susan, a girl in her twenties, casually dressed in jeans

Peter (*exhausted*) Oh, dear. Rather unfortunate.
Susan Sit over there.

Susan guides Peter to the bench and he sinks down on to it

This was a fairly silly idea.
Angie I didn't know the escalator would be broken.
Susan We could have gone back.
Angie We'd paid by then! You all right, Dadda...?
Peter Yes. Just let me get my breath.

Slight pause

Angie (*brightly*) Well, that was a lovely evening, wasn't it? (*Beat*) Till it went wrong.
Susan God.
Brian (*warning her*) Shut up, Susan.
Susan Didn't anybody else think it was frightful?
Angie I found it very nice.
Susan I can't stand a lot of bogus sentiment, being slowly drowned in warm treacle. I hate these films where the hero dies and keeps coming back in soft focus just to reassure everybody—chin up, chaps! Life is super in the supernatural afterland, God's in his heaven, and paradise has been designed by Walt Disney.

Angie (*hurt*) I thought it was beautiful.

Peter (*mildly*) A lot of people enjoyed it.

Susan Yes, that's what worries me.

Angie It was so warm and sincere, it had such a lovely message.

Susan I got the message, but the rest of you wouldn't leave.

Brian (*beginning to be irritated by her*) Oh, come on, Susan, it was a fun night out—what did you want to see?

Susan Reality. I don't know. Anything relevant—strong— something with edge and violence and life, something to do with the real world.

Peter Interesting. Why do you think violence is more real than gentleness? Louder, certainly; uglier, possibly—but more real?

Angie Yes, I'm sure that's very clever. What's the time, when are we ever going to get home...?

Brian Do you want me to check?

Angie Would you, Brian? Try and find someone in authority— and for heaven's sake don't get lost.

Brian exits through the arch L

I do like that boy. So helpful.

Peter He is hardly likely to get lost in the Underground.

Angie Oh, I don't agree: all those passages which look exactly alike, and whenever I'm by myself they always come out on the wrong platform. Did I ever tell you what happened to me in South Kensington?

Susan Yes.

Angie draws Susan DR

Angie (*vaguely worried; dropping her voice*) Dadda has had a good time really. Hasn't he?

Susan I expect so.

Angie You mustn't pay too much attention to what he says. He does like to sound terribly intelligent and make me seem a fool, but it's a game, of course. Both of us play a kind of little game with each other—when you're married you'll understand.

Susan (*in a low voice*) How ill is he?

Angie Oh, medical science can do such wonderful things.

Susan God.

Angie It's very important to be positive.

Susan So?

Angie They said angina. We don't talk about it.

Susan But he's only four years older than you are——

Angie Six years older.

Peter (*looking up suddenly; loudly*) I think I've lost my hat.

Both women turn up stage

Angie Oh Dadda, you haven't——

Susan Did you leave it in the cinema?

Peter Possibly.

Angie But you had it in your hand—did you put it down when you bought the train tickets? Stay here, both of you, I'll go and look...

Angie runs out through the arch L

Slight pause

Peter (*amiably*) Shall we argue?

Susan No. You're supposed to rest.

Peter Tell me about Brian.

Susan (*shrugging it off*) He's a young man.

Peter I had noticed.

Susan What do you want me to say? He's a student from the LSE, he's reading economics, he's good in bed, I find him amusing.

Peter (*curiously*) Is that what you lot look for?

Susan A sensible relationship. On equal terms, as honest intellectual partners. My grades are better than his.

Peter That must be very reassuring.

Slight pause

Susan Do you have to be so abrasive?

Peter I'm sorry.

Susan Listen, it's nothing to do with you; I'm not asking for your opinion——

Peter Good. To ask for my approval would be ridiculous; it is, finally, not my business. Nothing to do with me.

Susan No!

Slight pause

Peter You've been talking to Angie.

Susan Yes. So, as I've been told the truth, we can agree on one thing at least. It is nothing to do with you.

Liz suddenly jumps to her feet

Liz There's a train coming! (*She runs* DR *and peers off*)

Susan (*startled*) Oh no—— (*She runs* UL. *She calls*) Brian... Brian, there's a train...

Peter rises slowly from the bench

Peter Are you certain?

Liz Come down here, you can feel the wind.

Susan joins Liz DR. *They both stare off* R

Susan She's right. A rush of air. It must be coming down the tunnel.

Slight pause

Where is it?
Peter You ought to be able to see the lights by now.
Susan Only wind. And an awful sort of chemical smell.

Liz turns away UC

Liz False alarm, bloody hell, sorry.

Angie runs on through the arch L

Angie Have we missed it—has it gone—where's Brian?
Peter All right, Angie, calm down, we made a mistake.
Angie But I heard the train—just a moment ago…
Peter No, not a train, just wind from the ventilator. (*He sits slowly on the bench*)

Slight pause

Angie I can't find your hat. It would be the good one.
Liz (*conversationally*) Waiting gets you nervy, don't you think? All this hanging about. Here. Did you lot pass a bloke in the passage?
Angie Are you talking to me?
Liz A while back I could hear drums. Somebody playing the drums. I wondered, maybe there's a busker still around.

They are all staring at her

Some hope! Well. That's what I thought.

Angie (*irritably*) There ought to be a guard. An inspector. Someone in authority to tell us what's going on.

Susan We are waiting for a train. (*She moves away* DR)

Liz crosses UC *to Peter*

Peter (*looking up at Liz*) Where have you got to get to?

Liz A party.

Peter It's late.

Liz Yah, well, I haven't exactly got an invite, but this time of night nobody notices, do they? Only if it gets too late I suppose they'll all have left. Damn.

Peter I'd go home.

Liz Brilliant. Only trouble with that—it's three hundred miles away. Up north.

Peter (*eyeing her carrier bag*) Have you got a bed for the night?

Liz I get by.

Angie joins Susan DR

Angie (*in a low voice*) I wish he wouldn't do that.

Susan What?

Angie Talk to strangers. It's such a mistake to get involved. That sounds unkind—I don't mean to be unkind—but the first thing one thinks of these days is drugs. Violence. You have to be careful.

A soft, insistent drum beat begins off L. *They all react, looking off* L

Liz (*calling across to Angie*) See? I didn't make it up.

Susan Drums?

Peter It can hardly be drums. A piece of wood banging up against the wall. A metal bar broken loose and swinging in the wind.

Liz Oh, something on the track, yah. One of the rails cracked.
Creepy.
Angie It's coming from the passage.

Susan moves UL

Susan I'll go and look.

She goes to exit through the arch L

Angie No, don't—Susan, don't leave us, there's no need, it
doesn't matter. Susan, please be sensible——

But Susan is gone

Oh, dear.
Liz She might just as well find out. Don't you think? (*She slumps
down on the floor with her back against the wall* C)

The drum beat fades to silence

Angie It's stopped now. So stupid to bother. (*She moves* UC *to
Peter*) You all right, Dadda——
Peter Yes, of course. (*He reaches up and takes her hand*) Angie.
Angie What?
Peter I had a lovely evening. Thank you.

*Angie stands beside the bench, holding his hand. Liz, her knees
up, is resting her head on her arms. It is possible she means to go
to sleep again*

The Lights fade slowly to Black-out

In the Black-out the scene changes. The two posters are removed

and the signs above the arches reversed. "EXIT" is now L *and*
"NO EXIT" is R

When the Lights come up we are in a different part of the tunnel

Susan enters through the arch R

She crosses C, *and suddenly swings round as if hit*

Susan Don't do that, you fool! (*She puts her hand to her shoulder
and turns, puzzled to find no-one there*) Brian...? Brian!

Brian enters through the arch L

Brian You won't believe this. I got lost.
Susan (*angry and rather shaken*) How the hell did you get there?
Brian Crazy. I went down the wrong escalator and found myself
on the Northern line.
Susan Oh, don't play stupid games, I'm not in the mood. You
were behind me a minute ago.
Brian (*surprised*) What? I've just come through there. (*He
points to the arch* L)
Susan No, stop it, stop it, it's late and I'm tired. You followed me
down the passage.
Brian I didn't! Honestly. Susan——
Susan I could hear your footsteps. Echoing. You kept dodging
back round the bend and then you came up behind and grabbed
hold of my shoulder—it's silly and you can really upset people.
Brian But I didn't do it——
Susan Oh, grow up, I could feel you breathing on my neck.
Brian I was nowhere near you! I was walking down that blasted
escalator...

Slight pause

Susan (*faintly uneasy now*) Brian...

Brian (*beginning to be alarmed himself*) Someone followed you...?

Susan (*with an effort*) No. Of course not, only joking. (*Lightly*) Me and me technicoloured imagination. Sorry. (*She breaks away from him* DR)

Brian No, wait a minute. You said they grabbed hold of your shoulder.

Susan Touch of cramp.

Brian follows her DR

Brian Look. If there really was a man behind you, this could be serious—you might have been attacked——

Susan (*turning*) Oh, for God's sake—I said, I said. I didn't see anybody.

Brian Maybe he ran off because I got here...

Susan Right. Enter Batman, James Bond, and all three of the musketeers—just forget it, will you?

Slight pause

Coming back to reality. Have you found a porter, a ticket inspector, someone to ask?

Brian No. (*He moves away from her, irritated*) I suppose the damn station is still open.

Susan Yes. The lights are on and there are other people about— a few minutes ago we heard somebody banging a drum.

Brian (*turning to her*) You heard it too...?

Susan The drum, yes, but that doesn't prove life on earth.

Brian What?

Susan Peter suggested a trick of sound in the tunnel, a piece of metal hanging loose against the wall.

Brian (*deciding she is teasing him*) Good thinking, there's quite

a wind down here. (*He crosses and puts his arms round her*)
Kiss me before the ghoulies get us.

They kiss

Susan What a dear old fashioned sex maniac you are.
Brian (*kissing her*) Am I doing well?
Susan Expert.
Brian No, listen, how do I rate with your family?

Susan breaks away from him UC

Susan God knows. It's not important.
Brian I think your father likes me.

Susan sits on the bench and looks up at him

Susan Brian. Let's get something clear from the very start. It
doesn't matter a damn what Peter thinks. He's not my father.
Brian Oh. Sorry. Nobody said——
Susan Sooner or later, getting slightly pissed and a wee bit
sentimental, Angie is certain to tell you the whole sad story.
Brian (*faintly embarrassed*) Look. It's nothing to do with me.
Susan Angie was a teenage mum.
Brian (*definitely embarrassed*) Well, she wouldn't want you to
tell——
Susan Oh, but she would! Angie revels in the whole thing; time
stopped for Angie in the sixties. He was a pop star, would you
believe, my father was a pop star.
Brian Romantic.
Susan You're joking. He played for a group called The Dawn
Breakers, and don't pretend you've ever heard of them, be-
cause you haven't.
Brian Not my subject.

Susan The Dawn Breakers. He was called—or he called himself—Martin Valiant. Don't you find that rather hard to take?

Brian What's in a name.

Susan Oh, everything, when you've invented it yourself. The
complete give-away. Martin Valiant and the Dawn Breakers.
I nearly got christened Rosalie Dawn.

Brian What happened?

Susan Peter stopped it.

Brian So he...

Susan Yes, he was on the scene by then. In the nick of time. I have
a perfectly respectable legal father—and a real father. Sometimes I wish I could have talked to him. But when I look at his
photograph—leather jacket, gold chains, hair tied at the nape
of the neck with a small bow—I think: what the hell could we
have talked about?

Brian You've seen pictures of him.

Susan Oh, God, yes. Angie kept all his photos, press cuttings,
letters—and every single one of his records. She plays them
over and over again, behind locked doors. They're not very
good. Terribly derivative. They sound like every tune you've
ever heard from the sixties.

Brian Be fair. You're not musical.

Susan Or sentimental. Angie was. Angie followed Martin
everywhere until—surprise, surprise—she got pregnant. They
had a screaming row one night outside the Underground.

Brian Poor Angie.

Susan No, as it turned out, poor Martin. She ran yelling into the
station, he went in after her—and what followed was so
ludicrous. Absurd. Unnecessary. It was the rush hour, you see,
he tried to push past everybody else, caught his foot on the
escalator and fell. I've seen the newspaper reports; she keeps
even those. There must have been a kind of domino effect, the
escalator kept moving, the crowds kept pouring in, nobody

understood what had happened—within a minute fifty people were injured and three people were dead. Amongst them my father.

Brian Killed in the crush.

Susan What upset me—what always upsets me—I picture him as very extrovert, flamboyant, outrageous. So the end's all wrong, isn't it? To die in such a stupid way from one silly little accident. Martin Valiant. He should have died in character, from drugs or drink or a highly publicised suicide.

Brian Or not died at all.

Susan I wonder.

Slight pause

Brian Where does Peter come into it?

Susan (*still contemplating an imaginary life with Martin*) Who? Sorry?

Brian Peter.

Susan Oh, he rented a room from Angie's parents. He was some kind of minor schoolteacher in those days. He still is. But he married Angie.

Brian Happy ending.

Susan If you think so. Yes, she lives in a daydream of sentimental memories and he gets on with whatever interests him, I suppose. Poor Angie.

Brian Poor Peter.

Susan rises and crosses DR

Susan Oh, come on, people like that settle for whatever they can get. If I'd been Angie I would never have married Peter in a thousand years: I would have said "Sod you" and got a job. (*She moves impatiently* L) Listen, what are we going to do? Shall we try again for a taxi?

Brian We didn't have any luck last time and I honestly don't feel
your father—your step-father, or whatever—ought to hang
around in the rain. He's ill. It took ages to get him down here
and it'll take even longer to get him back up again.

Susan Damn.

Brian Do be reasonable.

Susan And kind? (*She mocks him*) You think I'm a bitch, don't
you?

Brian A bit thoughtless sometimes.

Susan turns on him

Susan The world has changed, Brian. You can't rely on the
endless sympathy of women any longer. I can't and won't get
entangled in family emotions—demands—expectations. I am
what I am—women don't have to pretend any more—smile
and smile and keep playing the hypocrite—what you see is
what you get. Sorry.

Brian I love you.

Susan I love you. At the moment.

They laugh as he kisses her

Brian Will you marry me?

Susan No.

Brian Why not?

Susan We're having too much fun. (*She breaks away from him*)

*A shadow appears on the back wall. Not very big. A shapeless
blur which shudders a little. Brian sees it*

And that's not completely selfish, lover; I don't want to stand
in your way either.

Brian is staring at the shadow

What are you looking at?

Brian (*puzzled*) That shadow. Where's it coming from? (*He crosses* UC *to examine the wall*)

Susan My point is, we both need to be free agents—Brian?

Brian I don't understand what's casting that shadow. (*He turns and peers off* R)

Susan I want a relationship based on honesty and respect—a real commitment——

Brian Look. There's a shadow. But there's nothing there to cast a shadow.

Susan You don't even listen, do you?

Brian Sorry.

Susan (*ironically*) Never mind, it's only women's talk.

Brian Susan——

Susan (*impatiently*) Oh, let's get back to the others. Everybody will think we're lost—come on.

Susan exits angrily through the arch L

After a second, Brian follows her, still looking over his shoulder at the wall, puzzled

The Lights begin to fade. Somewhere off R *a very soft drum begins to beat. The shadow moves slowly across the wall from* R *to* L

Black-out

In the Black-out the scene changes. The "EXIT" sign is moved to the arch R, *the "NO EXIT" sign to the arch* L. *The two posters are returned to the wall* C

We are now in the original tunnel

As the Lights come up, they reveal Liz in her crouching position against the back wall, fast asleep

Peter rises from the bench, rubbing his leg

Angie watches him anxiously

Angie You all right, Dadda?
Peter My foot's gone to sleep.
Angie It won't be much longer. Will it? We really shouldn't split up because any minute now there'll be a train. Won't there?

Slight pause

Wouldn't it be awful if they locked us in. I don't suppose there's really any chance they've locked us in.
Peter (*placidly*) I should think absolutely none.

Slight pause

Angie I must be a terrible nuisance to you.
Peter Calm down.
Angie I can't help being nervous. I don't enjoy being nervous, nobody wants to be nervous. Where have they got to? (*She calls*) Brian! Susan! (*She moves* UL) Oh, dear. (*She turns to him*) Do you like that boy?
Peter Well enough.
Angie He's still a student. He hasn't any money. I think they're sleeping together. I feel I ought to say something but I don't like to, it would be so embarrassing.
Peter I should leave them alone.

There is a sudden rattling drum beat off R—*harsh, staccato, loud. Liz wakes with a start*

Liz God Almighty!

Angie What was that…?

Peter A broken signal banging against the wall. A metal bar falling to the ground.

Liz struggles to her feet

Liz Bloody hell, what's going on?

Peter Nothing. Nothing. Nothing has happened.

Liz reaches for her carrier bag

Liz I want out. You lot coming?

Peter Two of us are missing.

Angie (*calling*) Susan! Brian! (*She crosses* R *to the arch*)

Liz crouches down, re-arranging the clothes in her carrier bag

Liz (*looking up at Peter*) I don't fancy being shut in. Specially underground. I expect I'm claustrophobic. Is that what I mean—I mean, claustrophobic?

Peter Where will you go?

Liz Some place else.

Peter Could I suggest the police station?

Liz (*rising*) Hey, what are you, a flaming social worker?

Peter No, I'm a flaming schoolteacher, but I still think you should go to the police station. I would take you, only I'm not very well. (*He sits back on the bench*)

Liz Sorry about that. What's wrong?

Peter I have heart trouble.

Liz Tough.

There is a sudden echoing crash off L*—a deafening roll of drums. Both Liz and Angie jump—and freeze, staring off* L

Oh, my God——

Peter (*calmly*) Vibration. An echo in the tunnel. They could be mending the line.

Angie I wish they'd get on with it, I wish somebody would come. (*She moves* UL *and stands in the archway, her back turned, gazing off* L)

Liz I got it. It's a radio. Somebody's down here with a transistor.

Peter I doubt if they work below ground.

Liz Why not? Look, get real, you heard it! That was a drum beat. Hey! You don't suppose they're having a rave party on the Northern line?

Peter I suspect the authorities would object.

Liz Stuff them.

Peter People used to shelter down here during the last war. Imagine. Whole families squatting on the platform—laughing, talking, singing, to keep their courage up. If you round a corner and see—almost see—rows of faces staring up at you, don't panic. It's only a shadow from yesterday's ghost.

Liz I don't know what you're on about and I don't believe in ghosts; I'm not silly. (*She stoops to pick up her carrier bag*)

Angie turns and moves DC

Angie This is ridiculous. Shall I go and look for them?

Peter No. For heaven's sake, if you start wandering about, we shall never find each other. Just stay put, Angie, they'll come back soon.

Liz crosses to the arch R *and hesitates*

Liz Here. I don't want to be a nuisance, but could you walk up to the entrance hall with me?

Angie Why?

Liz I don't like going down those empty passages on my own.

Angie Don't be stupid. There's nobody there.

Liz Yah, well, that's why, isn't it? I'm not scared, but I mean, what I mean, you could get attacked. This time of night. I'd be really grateful—if one of you could——

Angie (*tartly*) My husband certainly can't and I'm not going to. The escalator isn't working, by the way, so you'll have to use the stairs.

Peter If you're frightened, you can wait with us.

Angie Of course she isn't frightened; why should she be frightened? There's nothing to be afraid of, is there? It's just very irritating—and late—and I'm getting so tired. (*She sinks down on the bench beside Peter*)

Peter (*apologetically, looking at Liz*) I'm sorry.

Liz You go to hell.

Liz goes out through the arch R

Pause

Angie I'm not unkind. I don't mean to be—but you can't trust people any longer.

Peter I think she's run away from home.

Angie So do I, but does it matter: hundreds of these teenagers do it and they all make for London. It's very silly—I don't know why they come here.

Peter Looking for romance.

Angie Oh no, job hunting, don't you think? That generation have no use for romance. When you remember the sixties…

Peter I do remember the sixties. I used to feel like a guest who has been invited to the party by mistake.

Angie (*lost in her private dream*) The colour, the energy, the sheer excitement…

Peter The noise. Standing in a room and finding it quite impossible to have a conversation.

Angie And the clothes! There's no real fashion any more...

Peter I wish I'd been born fifty years earlier. Edwardian days would have been nice—so many giants of literature.

Brian enters through the arch L

Brian Susan, wait for me, I think we ought to... (*He breaks off, not seeing her*) Susan...

Peter She hasn't come this way.

Echoing footsteps can be heard off R

Brian She must have done. She was just ahead of me in the tunnel, I heard her footsteps.

Angie (*rising*) Yes. There she is, she's in the other passage. Susan! We're here, darling...

Angie and Brian cross to the arch R

Brian No.

The footsteps stop

She's taken the wrong turning.

Peter Don't you charge off again. Susan will find us. Nothing is gained by multiple hysteria. (*He takes a paperback book out of his pocket and begins to read it*)

Angie Nobody there. Well, that's your fault, you should have kept together.

Brian We did. I was following her, there were a lot of tunnels, but I don't see how I could have missed. Look. Susan and I agreed to give it up—we can't hang around here any longer.

Angie draws Brian DL

Angie (*in a low voice*) I realize you're tired—so am I—but it's very difficult with Dadda on our hands. I try to look after him, Brian, I really do. You probably find him boring and a bit of a nuisance—he's not had much of a life, he never got a proper job because of his health, and now there's nothing left except this rather dreary school, and they don't think much of him there. Only, I wouldn't want you to dismiss him as useless. The point is, Brian, you really mustn't judge Peter——

Brian I don't.

Angie You're very sympathetic. Are you serious about Susan?

Brian I doubt if she's interested in me.

Angie Oh, my dear, you mustn't say that; you've no idea how powerful real love can be. I've been lucky. You see, someone fell in love with me once. He's dead, but I still have memories.

Brian (*highly embarrassed*) It's a comfort.

Angie I think perhaps I ought to explain. If you have any doubts about Susan—Dadda isn't her father.

Brian So I understand.

Angie Oh, she told you, I'm so glad. He was called Martin. Martin Valiant. He was a drummer with The Dawn Breakers group. He would have been famous—oh, the crowds that used to follow Martin! He was killed in an accident.

Brian I'm sorry.

Angie Such a terrible waste, don't you think, all that life and talent! And he loved me.

Brian (*edging away from her*) Look, the moment Susan comes, I feel we ought to go.

Angie You're nice. I hope she marries you; her father would have been so happy. Do you think he knows—I think he knows. Sometimes I get the most warm and comforting feeling, as if I'm protected. I'm sure there's another world, aren't you?

Brian (*even more embarrassed*) I'm not religious, Mrs Leyland.

Angie Never mind. I'm sure you believe in something—everybody does—and what I believe, wherever Martin is, he must be feeling guilty and unhappy; he wants to make it up to me. I wish you'd known him. He was wonderful—exciting, romantic— the sun came out when Martin was there. Martin. My love. (*She crosses* DR, *lost in some private dream*)

Brian moves UC *to Peter*

Peter (*without looking up*) Is Angie upset? She probably thinks this is the station where he was killed.

Brian No.

Peter Actually it is.

Brian (*rather startled*) What?

Peter Only joking. Only joking.

Brian Oh. She does seem to believe the ghost of someone called Martin Valiant watches over her.

Peter I doubt it. He was a competitive and egotistical little bastard.

Brian, surprised, glances quickly at Angie, but she has obviously not heard

Brian Really, sir, you shouldn't——

Peter I beg your pardon. I'm so sorry, I thought your generation was supposed to be unshockable. *Mea culpa. De mortuis nil nisi bonum.* Did you have a classical education?

Brian I'm afraid not, but I know that one. Don't speak ill of the dead.

Peter Yes. Absolute nonsense, of course. I frequently speak ill of the dead; some of them thoroughly deserved it.

Brian What was his music like?

Peter Very loud. The tumbling rumble of drums. Staccato crackle.

Brian Not your style.

Peter Angie had all his records long before she met him. She
would play them over and over, late into the night. I used to
knock on her bedroom door and ask her to give silence a
chance—I was trying to work, you see. Sometimes she was
nice about it. Sometimes she wasn't.

Slight pause

Brian Could you manage the stairs, sir? We can't wait any
longer.

Peter Are you tired?

Brian Well, it's past midnight. It's too late for a train now.
They'll throw us out soon.

Angie turns and moves UC

Angie I'm cold. It's that wind. It's that wind again.

Brian Try walking up and down. The moment Susan gets back
we can——

There is a single violent scream off L. *Angie and Brian spin round.
There is a single loud bang off* L

What the hell——

Angie (*in total panic*) *No!* Susan—No, no, no…

Angie and Brian rush out through the arch L

Peter Extraordinary. And quite useless. (*He picks up his book
and begins to read*)

The Lights start to fade. A shadow appears on the wall UR.

Slithery, greyish, a formless shape, but rather bigger than it was before. It begins to move slowly from R *to* L, *shuddering a little*

Black-out

In the Black-out the scene changes as before. The signs over the arches are reversed and the posters taken down

When the Lights come up we are in the other part of the tunnel

  Brian and Angie rush on L

Brian It was through here——
Angie It wasn't, it wasn't—you keep going the wrong way——
Brian We should have gone to the left.
Angie No, I told you, I could hear her over on the right. Susan! Susan!

Somewhere off R *a very soft drum begins to beat*

  Oh, God. Listen.
Brian What?
Angie Martin.
Brian That is not a drum. That is vibration in the tunnel—your husband did explain.

There is a single violent scream off R

  Liz rushes through the arch R *and hurls herself into Brian's arms*

Liz (*screaming*) There's something there! Go away, go away——
Brian Don't—for heaven's sake—you're all right——

Liz It's coming——

Angie What is it? What's the matter with her?

Liz (*sobbing*) Can't you see it? Make it go away!

Brian Stop this! Now calm down. There's nobody here except
Mrs Leyland and me. Look.

He takes Liz by the shoulders and turns her round

Nothing. Is there?

Angie It's just your imagination. (*To Brian*) I expect she got lost.

Liz breaks away from Brian

Liz Yah. OK. Say it, say it. I'm a crazy case. All the same. I had
a bloody awful shock.

Angie Make her sit down.

Brian Come on. Don't worry. Over here.

*Brian guides Liz to the bench, makes her sit and then sits beside
her. The drum beat fades*

Tell me what happened.

Liz I felt all cold, suddenly. There was an odd kind of musty
smell. I couldn't find the way out! And then a mist come up the
stairs, whirring round and round, making for me——

Brian There's a wind in the tunnel. Probably dust.

Liz It went right through my body, it felt damp and smelt of rotten
apples.

Angie You'd better stay with us. (*To Brian. In a low voice*) Has
she been taking anything? Because if it's drugs, I don't know
what to do about that.

Liz rises

Liz (*with a sudden change of tone*) Get me! Ever so sorry, I must have given you a fright, I mean, what I mean, I had a real attack of the shivers.

Brian Never mind, just relax——

Liz Comes of being highly strung, nervous, you know—put it down to the weather, I would. Bye. (*She moves* L)

Angie Where are you going——

Liz Bloody hell out of here.

Liz exits L

Angie Ought we to——

Brian No.

Angie If she's ill——

Brian Let her go.

Angie (*looking through the* UL *arch*) She's gone down the wrong passage. She's going to get lost again.

Brian Tough.

Angie Brian...

Brian I got a strong impression that kid was play acting.

Angie Pretending? Oh no! To frighten us?

Brian Swirling mist and damp and peculiar smells; she's been seeing too many horror movies.

Slight pause

Angie Now, that is unforgivable. Horrid little bitch. How dare she? It's not fair, I was feeling bad enough without stupid practical jokes. I don't understand. Children used to be nice.

Brian She's not a child.

Angie That's what I mean. Young. But not a child.

Susan enters through the arch R

Susan What sort of silly game are you two playing?

Brian Susan——

Angie And what happened to you. (*She swings round, now more irritated than frightened*)

Susan I've been going round and round for ages.

Brian I was behind you! You managed to disappear——

Susan You were in front of me! I heard you calling from the top of the escalator.

Brian You can't have done. I wasn't there. I kept following the sound of your footsteps——

Susan You called "Susan". I heard you. "Susan. Susan."

Brian I didn't. This is ridiculous, we've just had a hysterical scene with that teenager who decided to play tricks on us…

Susan Was she screaming? I heard someone scream.

Brian We thought that was you.

Angie Oh, stop it, stop it! Please, can we find Dadda and go home?

Slight pause

Susan Yes.

Brian Yes.

Susan (*being rational*) Sound is difficult to place when you're underground.

Brian (*being rational*) I did call you from one of the passages.

Susan I expect that was it. I'm sorry, Angie. Shall we go?

They all go out through the arch L

An insistent drum beat begins off R. The Lights begin to fade. A shadow appears on the back wall. It is now much larger but still a formless blur. It moves slowly from R to L, shuddering

Black-out

In the Black-out the scene changes as before

When the Lights come up we are in the first section of the tunnel

>*Peter is sitting on the bench, placidly reading his paperback book*

>*Angie, Brian and Susan come in through the arch* L

Angie ...what I don't understand is why they all have to be so unkind. Dadda tells me some of the children in his class are quite impossible to control. We're going, Dadda.

Peter (*closing his book*) You found each other, then.

Susan (*kissing him*) Hallo. I gather I caused a panic.

Brian We heard a scream.

Susan I told you, it was your teenager playing tricks.

Peter Sound is indestructible—there's a thought for you. A scream goes on for ever, echoing through the universe, pursued by other screams and still more multiplying fears.

Angie You always choose the wrong time to be clever—it's awfully easy to laugh when other people are frightened.

Peter I'm sorry, Angie. *Mea culpa.*

Angie Yes, we all know you speak Latin. No, that's wrong, isn't it—you read Latin. I could never make out why anyone has to teach Latin at all; I mean, once a language is dead does it really matter what anybody said in it?

Peter Yes.

Susan When they were building the Underground they found a Roman mosaic. Did any of you know that? Correction. Do any of you care?

Peter Enlighten us. Ghostly Roman legions...

Susan Why not? Tramping soldiers and cursing generals—and Gaul is divided into three parts.

Peter No, my dear, a very common mistake in translation. Gaul—taken as a whole—is divided into three parts.

Susan It's the same thing.

Peter It is not.

Brian (*impatiently*) Come on, we've got six flights of stairs to climb. Can I give you a hand, Mr Leyland?

Angie freezes, staring off R

Angie What's that…?

Susan joins Angie DR

Susan What's the problem this time?

Angie There's a man standing in the tunnel. Isn't there…?

Susan (*peering off*) Shadows. Only flickering light.

Peter (*mildly*) There would hardly be a man in the middle of the railway track.

Angie Look—he moved——

Peter And if there were he'd be very dead by now.

Brian joins Angie and Susan DR

Brian It could be a workman. They're having trouble with the signals.

Susan The current is still on.

Brian Is it?

Susan Can't you hear, all around us, the hum of electricity, that odd chemical smell?

Peter They need power, I believe. Curious. I wonder if they squabble over the source of energy?

Susan Who do?

Peter The surging mass of ghosts. Your Romans—air raid families—workers, travellers, the victims of every accident——

Angie swings round and turns on him

Angie (*shrilly*) No! How can you—you're so stupid, insensitive—why bring that up, as if I'd forgotten, as if I didn't care!
Susan (*in a low voice*) Oh, God. Now you've done it. (*She breaks away* DL)
Peter I'm sorry, Angie. That was a stupid mistake.
Susan Yes.
Angie You don't even remember. But I remember. Martin. Martin.
Peter Come here, Angie. Forgive me, please.

Peter reaches for her hand but she pulls away from him

Angie It doesn't matter. You're not important enough to forgive. You don't count.
Peter That's true, I suppose. What a dreadful comment on one's life.

There is a sudden deafening crash of drums off R *and they all leap, staring off* R

Angie (*screaming*) Aaaaaaah!

Silence

Susan Something fell. Somewhere, something fell. No big deal. (*She crosses and puts her arms round Angie*) It's all right, Angie. All right. All right. (*To Peter, across Angie's shoulder*) You bloody fool.
Brian Workmen in the tunnel.
Susan Don't cry. You mustn't be frightened.
Angie (*clinging to Susan*) Will he come back?
Susan What?

Angie (*almost in a whisper*) Suppose Martin came back.

Susan (*losing patience*) Martin is dead.

Angie Yes. Only I keep imagining. If—out of the tunnel—I saw—— (*She clutches Susan in rising panic*) I don't want to see him! No, please, no, I don't want to see him again——

Susan You won't. You can't.

Angie (*shrilly*) Make him go away from me——

Susan He isn't there! For God's sake calm down!

Angie (*covering her face with her hands*) Go away, go away, I'm frightened——

Peter (*suddenly; loudly*) Angie!

This has the effect of a slap in the face. Angie breaks away from Susan. After a second, she turns, looking at them

Angie Yes. I'm so sorry. You must remember I'm the stupid one here.

Peter rises and goes DR to her, moving rather faster than he managed before

Peter We shall be home soon. (*He puts an arm round her*)

Angie Yes, of course.

Peter Hold on to me. You're safe.

Angie Peter. I have tried. I wish you'd understand that.

Peter I do.

Angie But I never got it right, did I? When I gave you a birthday present I'd see you glance at Susan—and I knew it was something you didn't want at all.

Peter You're wrong. Actually.

Angie You and Susan always snap at each other, and still you'd rather talk to her than me.

Peter I like talking to anybody.

Angie Even him?

Peter You couldn't talk to Martin. He was either playing his drums or conducting a monologue.

Angie It's not as if I believe in ghosts, you know, or survival. I used to think—like to think—because it was comforting. If he really came back I'd be terrified.

Peter Martin is not going to—— (*He gives a sudden gasp and puts a hand to his chest*)

Angie (*alarmed*) Dadda...? Was that one of the pains? Sit down—please—take my hand—slowly...

Angie guides Peter back to the bench, where he sits, exhausted

Susan Somebody will have to get a taxi. Brian——

Brian Yes, of course. Are you lot going to wait down here?

Susan See if it's raining. It might beat standing in a doorway.

Brian Right. It may take some time to raise a cab, so don't expect miracles.

Susan spins round abruptly

Susan (*sharply*) Let go of me!

Brian Sorry?

Susan I hate being pawed, just leave me alone.

Brian I wasn't near you.

Angie (*calling across*) Can we move? Dadda isn't feeling well.

Susan (*to Brian; angrily*) You were stroking my hair, now it's in a mess——

Brian I didn't touch you, Susan——

Susan I felt your hands sliding across my head. Don't do it.

Brian Yes, well, that's impossible; don't be silly.

Susan Why are you pretending? What are you saying—there's someone else here?

Brian No, of course there isn't——

One corner of a poster peels very slowly away, and hangs half down leaving a bare patch of the wall. (See production note.) They all gaze at it, rather shaken. Brian is the first to find his voice

That's caused by the atmosphere. The air becomes too warm and the poster dries out.

Peter gives a slow hand clap

(*Irritatedly*) It's possible!

Peter Yes. We will not examine the scientific basis of that. Well done.

Susan They don't put them up properly. For God's sake.

Angie I don't understand? Who did that, what's happening?

Peter All right, Angie.

Angie (*making an effort*) I'm not bothered. Are you all right?

Peter Thank you. (*Looking round them*) A taxi...

Brian Of course. It may take some time—no, I tell you what. I've got a minicab number. You wait, I'll find a telephone box in the booking hall and ring—— (*He puts his hand to his breast pocket, and freezes*) Bloody hell!

Angie Brian?

Brian That little bitch has nicked my wallet!

There is a pause. Then Susan bursts out laughing

Susan I'm sorry. I'm sorry, I find this hilarious. We're getting steamed up about ghostly apparitions and all we've met is a very real pickpocket.

Brian (*furiously*) I'll damn well get her. (*He moves rapidly* UL)

Susan You won't. You can't. Oh, come here, you lunatic, she's miles away by now.

Brian No. She took the wrong passage. With a bit of luck she's lost herself down the corridors—if I can't find her, I'm going to the police.

Brian exits through the arch L

Slight pause

Peter (*placidly*) Does he mean to come back?

Susan Yes. In a minute.

Angie (*bemused by the speed of events*) Oh, dear. His wallet? How did she manage?

Susan By screaming she'd seen a ghost and hurling herself into his arms. It's an old trick.

Angie But that's dreadful. Had he got a lot of money?

Susan I've no idea.

Peter Judging by his excitement, quite a lot.

Susan Have you noticed how we stop worrying about the supernatural when we lose solid cash? Poor Brian. No ghost. Just a tatty little teenage crook.

Angie I can hear him.

Susan What?

There is a sound of slow footsteps approaching off L

Angie In the passage. Thank goodness.

Susan crosses UL

Susan (*calling*) Any luck, Brian?

The footsteps grow louder, closer

I can't see him.

Angie runs UL *and looks through the arch*

Angie He's coming now——

The footsteps stop

Susan No.

Angie But he's there, he must be, I heard his footsteps——

Peter The nature of sound——

Susan (*turning, irritated*) I know, I know, sound is indestruct-
    ible, you told us. God, this place must be full of over-lapping
    noises.

Peter Marching Romans, medieval workmen, tunnelling axes,
    hurrying commuters, falling bombs. Immeasurable layers.
    World upon world, each one wiping out the world beneath it.

Susan All right. What do you suggest? A Roman ghost stalking
    the passages?

Peter Why not? It's just as likely as any other. Only the vanity
    of the present persuades you it must be Martin, it must relate to
    you.

Angie Martin? Is Martin here?

Susan No, of course he isn't.

Angie (*sliding into panic*) You said it wasn't possible, you said
    there couldn't be ghosts, people don't come back——

Susan (*suddenly*) Be quiet.

There is a sound of slow footsteps approaching off R

    Now it's in the other tunnel.

Peter Walls pick up an echo. The source could be anywhere.

Susan But it's over on the right now. (*She moves* UR *to examine
    the arch* R)

The footsteps stop

Silence

Gone.
Angie (*shakily*) Dadda. Get me out of here. Please.

A soft insistent drum beat begins off L. *Susan spins round and moves* UL *to the arch* L

Susan I'm not going to argue about this. That's a drum.
Peter If you think so.
Angie Martin played the drums. It sounds so like Martin. That's what you mean. That's what you're saying.
Peter The Romans had drums. So had the Greeks.
Susan (*angrily*) Oh, God, you're so unsubtle. Talk away, change the subject, keep the women amused.
Peter (*mildly*) *Mea culpa.*
Susan (*savagely*) And when in doubt, trot out one of the little Latin tags you wear round your neck as proof of good breeding.
Peter Shall I apologize in English?
Susan It would be a help if you...

The drum beat stops. Susan spins round, startled

Don't!
Peter (*eyeing her*) Susan?
Susan (*shaken, but determined to hide it*) Don't--we mustn't--we shouldn't go on like this; we're upsetting Angie. (*She moves* DR, *one hand to her head*)
Peter (*curiously*) Did something touch your hair just then?

Susan brings her hand away abruptly

Susan No. I think I've lost a hair grip. Damn.
Peter Don't be afraid.

Susan (*facing him; angrily*) I'm not! I am cold and tired, and I am going to get a taxi—we can't just hang around waiting for Brian. (*She moves to the arch* R)

Angie (*in panic*) Don't go——

Peter All right. All right. What we'll do. Susan, you and Angie go up to the booking hall. When you have got a taxi, Susan can hang on to it, and Angie can come back down and collect me.

Angie No! We must all stay together.

Peter I'm sorry. I'm afraid I can't do it, I really can't keep up with the rest of you. I would far rather just sit here. You won't be long.

Angie joins Susan UR, *torn between her urge to escape and her anxiety for Peter*

Angie (*looking back; doubtfully*) Dadda...? (*To Susan*) Ought we to leave him on his own?

Susan (*to Peter*) Are you sure? Is this what you want?

Peter Oh yes.

Angie It isn't that I'm thoughtless or stupid; only, honestly, if something went wrong, I wouldn't be any use——

Susan Don't worry. Brian will turn up again in a minute, and we must get home.

Susan and Angie exit through the arch R

Peter picks up his book and begins to read. The drum beat begins again off L. *The shadow appears on the back wall. It is now much larger—a shuddering grey blur, never completely in focus*

Peter (*without looking up*) Yes. I know you're there, Martin. (*He puts down his book, looks up, and starts to laugh, very softly*) Extraordinary. It seems that death does not enlighten you.

The drum beat swells. The shadow grows larger

You see. The fact is. She's not your daughter, Martin. She's mine.

The drum beat stops. The shadow freezes—quivering. Still

I'm afraid Angie was two months pregnant when she met you. But a sickly little schoolteacher who rented a room from the family—it wouldn't do. It didn't fit the romantic, the necessary dream.

The drum beat begins again, staccato, agitated. The shadow moves towards him, swelling in size

I think I have been reasonably tolerant. A fair bargain, on the whole. Angie had her dream and I—oh, I had my halo of virtue, the long-suffering friend in need. I was much admired.

The shadow is nearly on him now. Peter tries to rise by leaning back against the wall and pushing himself upright

But I must make one thing clear. You are not to come near my daughter, Martin.

The drum beat grows louder, faster, more and more agitated. Peter's voice rises in open triumph

She's mine, Martin! Mine! She's mine, she's mine, Martin——

The shadow falls across him. There is a resounding crash of drums—discordant, violent

Black-out

Silence

The Lights creep back on very slowly

Peter is sitting on the bench, leaning back, apparently peacefully asleep

Liz enters through the arch L

Seeing Peter alone, she moves cautiously over to him. As there is no movement, her hand steals towards his breast pocket, feeling for the wallet—and she recoils in shock. She spins round and rushes to the arch R

Liz (*frightened; calling*) Will somebody help, please—can somebody come—will somebody help——

Liz holds her position in the arch as the Lights fade

CURTAIN

FURNITURE AND PROPERTY LIST

On stage: Vividly coloured posters
Red plastic bench
"EXIT" sign
"NO EXIT" sign

Personal: **Liz**: bulging carrier bag. *In it:* clothes
Peter: paperback book

LIGHTING PLOT

Property fittings required: nil
2 interior settings

To open: Harsh and flat, slightly orangey general lighting

Cue 1   **Liz** rests her head on her arms   (Page 9)
       Slowly fade to black-out

Cue 2   When ready   (Page 10)
       Lights up to opening state

Cue 3   **Susan** breaks away from **Brian**   (Page 15)
       Project a shadow on the back wall

Cue 4   **Brian** exits   (Page 16)
       Slowly fade lights

Cue 5   Soft drum begins to beat   (Page 16)
       The shadow moves slowly across the wall, R *to* L;
         then black-out

Cue 6   When ready   (Page 17)
       Lights up to opening state

Cue 7   **Peter** starts to read his book   (Page 24)
       Slowly fade lights; project a shadow on the
       back wall, bigger than before, moving R *to* L;
       then fade to black-out

Cue 8   When ready   (Page 25)
       Lights up to opening state